Loved Beyond My Issues…
Lyrically Free To Be Me

Authored by:
Simply Stacy

Illustrated By:
Sydney Wilson

Loved Beyond My Issues…
Lyrically Free To Be Me

Printed in the United States of America.

ISBN: 978-0-9887188-2-1

This one is for my Lord and Savior Jesus Christ… He literally freed me to be me… My husband, Jelani, my children, Terrell, Sydney and Joi… thank you for hanging in there with me while I trek through this process to walk out God's purpose for me.

BOOM! Here we go…

Table of Contents

LOVED

Eternal.... HAIKU
Today Tomorrow
Forever together we
Will love endlessly

Love Realized

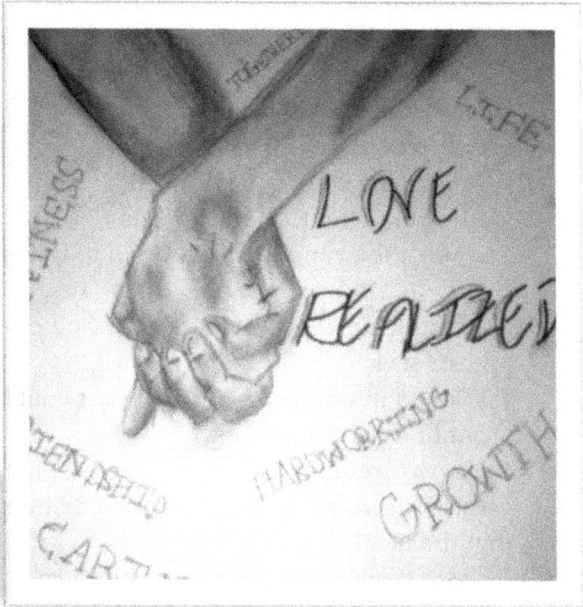

I went looking for love in all the wrong places
Looking for affirmation by way of forced
smiling faces
Gave negativity, insecurity, pain free of rent
spaces in my heart…
Not realizing I needed to know God, to
understand Love
I made the choice to know Him
Allowing Him to show me, me
It was then you see, that I begin to understand
Love
After all He was the epitome of the Love my
heart seek
I would never see Love for what it could be
until I begin to see God
He was strategic too
Introduced me to Agape… Love that hit me
in the heart
This was the Love that was hardest to
comprehend
God had to help me understand that Agape
Love was pure love from Him
Storge Love, this love was natural for me…
the love I have for my family
God helped me to see that Love comes in
many forms
Forms you choose and forms that choose
you… all you need to do is have your heart
open to receive
Then He introduced me to Phileo love… love
where I made the choice…

Affectionate, platonic, fondness in the heart, friendship
Finally God showed me that my heart was ready to receive
Eros love… passionate, intense love
That often we think we need over anything
I learned that God is a God of order indeed
By way of how He grew me in Love
He had to show me that He needed to take lead
In order for me to see the true love intended for me
Now, I'm able to give, sacrificially to all that I love
Even learned how to love strangers
Understanding and being at peace
Knowing my heart wasn't in danger
That when LOVED beyond me…
I was loving Godly
I didn't find Love… Love found me
Love rounded my circle
Made it complete!

Looking For Love

There are so many misunderstandings when it comes to Love. As a woman, I know my biggest misunderstanding when it came to Love was thinking I needed passionate (Eros) love to be completed as a woman. Now, Eros love is DEFINITELY a need and desire… but I had the order ALL WRONG! I didn't really know who I was, I didn't take the time to allow myself to be healed from the hurt of a past relationship before I was on the hunt for another relationship. In my mind, I thought the new love would heal the hurt from the old love.

I didn't realize God was the only One Who could heal my hurt heart; nor did I realize the hurt I carried from my past would infect my present. The cycle began and before I knew it, my heart was tattered and then I started questioning my worthiness for a passionate love relationship. I didn't even pay attention to the fact that I was so broken I didn't know how to love on any level effectively. God did a complete re-work on my heart, lots of digging and removing.

He showed me Him, His Power, and helped me understand that I needed to know Him and through knowing Him, accepting His love for me, I would learn to love me. Ha! Who knew that I didn't love me all that time? Hard but necessary pill to swallow, but once I got it down… it all went up from there for me. I learned to accept God's love for me, love myself, and found myself loving my friends better, my family better and even being able to demonstrate love for my fellow man sincerely. One of the greatest turn arounds in this journey called Love for me, was being FOUND by the man God intended for me.

My biggest mistake in the journey of Love was me looking for the passionate love I desired. I DID NOT understand that all I needed to do was get ready, be ready and positioned and I would be found. That "be ready" stance was a substantial amount of work. I didn't need to be perfect because he wouldn't be perfect, but I did need to be healed, fully secure in who I was, love God and love me before the "he" I desired would find me. He literally did not see me until I arrived to that place of being prepared. I am still on this journey called love… I struggle to this day with loving those who hurt me… but I'm better than what I was. If you're reading this, please know, you don't need to look for Love, love found you, Love created you, Love is waiting for you to accept His love for you so that He can show you Love on every level you desire and need.

Whole Armor

We…we have to be strong!
Strong in The Lord and in the Power of His
might.
You can't fight this thing alone
God is needed every day of your life.
Put on the whole armor of God!
So that you may be able to stand…
Against the wiles of the devil and every tool
he attempts to use to derail you.
Remember, we don't wrestle against flesh and
blood… it is often people that he uses too, to
upset, confuse and take the best from you!
Fight spirit with Spirit, we war against
principalities, powers, rulers of the darkness
of this age, and more importantly we war
against host of wickedness in heavenly places.
Therefore, take up the whole armor of God
that you may be able to withstand the evil day,
and having done all to stand.
Stand! Man Stand! Woman…
Your waist girded with Truth
The breastplate of righteousness, sure looks
good on you!
Shod those feet with the preparation of the
Gospel of Peace.
Take that shield of faith, blocking the fiery
fleet of darts the enemy will attempt to send
your way!
The helmet of salvation covers the crown of
your head and the sword of the Spirit, God's
Word is how you're led.

Keeping prayer on your lips and deep in your
heart!
Dressing yourself with the Whole Armor of
God wins the battles before it even starts!
Before you get your coffee
Child, before you get out of that bed!
Put on the Whole of Armor of God
Ensure you're covered from the bottom of
your feet to the top of your head!

You're Protected

*We are guaranteed struggles in this life, but we can
have peace. God wants to give us Peace of mind, peace
in living, and even Joy in the midst of all we will face.
Here's the interesting point about that, you have to
choose to want what God has for you. The Whole
Armor of God, equips you to deal with everyday life
hurdles and you find hope in knowing that God is
with you. You can overcome the pains of life and enjoy
each day you're given with God's protection. Choose
Him, He won't disappoint you.*

Scriptural Reference Ephesians 6:10-18

The Evolution of Love

My heart grows
With every single beat there it goes
This phenomenon
Can only be
Due to the way
That you love me
Seeded by honesty
Fertilized by trust
Watered by communication
Deep rooted
Nurtured love
Far beneath my skin
Touching parts of my soul
When we come in contact
This love, reveals stories untold
Kisses brand new
Hugs, two are never the same
Words spoken take flight
The kind of love, that makes you look
forward…
To the coming days
This love does indeed exists
It's not a myth
Happily ever after may not always be the case
Instead, real love, progressive love
The kind of love that takes shape
Love that heals
Looking past the insecurities
Finding the essence of each heart involved
Love… EVOLVED

Fairy Tale Faux Pas

I don't believe in fairy tales, not even as a little girl, I never believed in them, but I did have an unrealistic expectation of what love was. I wanted love, just like everyone else, I wanted sweet kisses, soft words, cuddling on cold and rainy days, but I couldn't see past that. I entered into love relationships with the expectation of perfection, not thinking, "Ummm Stacy, you're not perfect," and when the hurdles of the relationship came into place, I wasn't ready... I tumbled, fumbled and ended up hurt.

I'd been hurt so much that my heart was hardened to the idea of true love. I had to go through healing for my hurt, but at the same time I had to come to an understanding that true love does not come without imperfection and working beyond the imperfections is a part of the love relationship. Once I learned and grew beyond my painful experiences, I was blessed with the gift of a sincere love relationship. I won't lie, it hasn't been easy and even in all I learned, I almost lost it all... one thing I fully understand now, more than ever, "What God has blessed, NO MAN (not even myself) can put asunder." Enduring the really rough patch in my relationship, trusting God fully for its complete renewal, beyond restoration, I was able to experience "God working what was meant for my bad out for my good."

Today, I'm enjoying love, reciprocal love, and imperfect but growing love. He and I become better with each trial we grow beyond. It's a two-way street, communication is required, prayer, trust in God, and selflessness is a must. True love exists, it's real and people deserve it. Sincere, heartfelt, mind changing, spirit growing love is attainable. There's nothing super special about me that justifies the earthly love I've been given, if God did it for me… He can, He wants to do more for you!

A Cleaned Up Mess

Lord knows I have made a mess
Messed up mouth
Messed up mind
Wouldn't be surprised that when Jesus comes
back
He leaves me behind…
Wouldn't be anyone's fault but mine
After all, the messes I've made
No one to blame
I won't drop one name
With my head hung in shame
I take full responsibility for the mess that is
me
Ready to wallow and live with my pain
You opened my eyes wide
Told me to trust Your plan
You wash away my shame
All I have to do is trust You, grow, pray and
embrace the change
My pain, my shame, hung with You on that
cross
Where I was ready to wear sorrow
You showed me that hope was not lost
This mess that I am, I no longer have to be
Choosing to Love and serve You
Cleans me up daily
Now, all that God sees when He sees me
Is clean, delivered and free
I'm refocused, living this life
Seeing myself
As You see me

You Messed Up…Fessed Up…God Blessed Up

When you first get saved, you're so excited that you go ALL IN! There is often a cycle the believer goes through, getting comfortable in your salvation is one of those cycles and that's where we really start slipping up. I don't know about you, but it was hard for me to bounce back from those tough falls that resulted in me getting comfortable with God. I really didn't take it serious that I was in a race of faith, when you understand that, you realize, the runner doesn't stop running the race because they're at a comfortable pace.

One thing you can count on with God, once you've trusted Him with your life, even when you mess up, if you come back, sincerely remorseful and seeking change, He takes what was meant for your bad and turns it around for you good. There is no mess up too messy for God to clean up. Yes, the enemy will try to remind you of your mess ups when you get back on track but you take solace in knowing what God says trumps what the enemy says EVERY TIME! You fell off track? It's as easy to get back on track as getting down on your knees!

Mirror's View

Hey there you, in the mirror's view
Welcome to a new day
Your eyes, don't just love them?
Big and bright
Hold on to your hope
It's the fuel that drives you through life
Enjoy this view, of you
Beautiful indeed
Don't forget to trust God
In Him, you'll always have everything you
need
That face, that smile, those too
Take a moment, my friend
Embrace the mirror's view

Do You Love Who You Are?

Society's opinion shouldn't hold so much weight in our individual lives, especially since we don't know who "society" is, but it has. Today, it's "cool" to have posi-vibes and "love yourself." I have a question for those of you taking time out to read this, "How do you define self-love?" Society's definition is surface, but self-love is much deeper. Loving yourself fully, consists of accepting your imperfections, physical, spiritual, and emotional. Loving yourself includes enjoying who you are, who you've grown into, where you came from. There are levels to loving yourself, just like there are levels to loving others. Loving yourself impacts your ability to love others. We've all heard the saying, "How can you expect someone to love you when you don't love yourself?" That's an easy question to ask, but the journey to truly loving who you are, first starts with allowing yourself to be healed, you have to allow God to show you how He sees you. You have to believe that what He created when He created you, was beautiful from the moment you were breathed into existence.

I learned that loving myself required me not to believe that I had to be what "society" deemed beautiful, successful, or the right type. Loving myself started with me believing what God said about me and working toward growing even more in Him. I had to embrace the things that I once labeled bad about myself and the biggest and most important characteristic I'm glad I accepted is my originality! You're unique on purpose, you're supposed to be different, do different, see different, embrace your differences and love YOU!

BEYOND

Boxed In HAIKU
I don't have the skills
Now is not the time to start
I'll wait one more day

Used

He died for me
Yet I hide from Him
He bled for me
Yet I won't stand to my feet to reverence His
Name
Often, He's taken for granted
His faithfulness and promise to never leave
used as license to abuse
Oh, but what would I do if God decided to
do the same to me?
Blessed me based on how much I give
Struck me down because of how I live?
When will we get tired of using Him?
What if He got tired of loving us?
Questions we don't ask, because we know
He's not like man
His faithfulness toward us, we can't
understand.
He gets tired too
He wants more from you
He gives to an undeserving you
Only to be left, used
Doesn't that bother you?

Grace Abounds

I am most certainly guilty of Grace Abuse indeed. I believe I've reaped some things from that abuse… but even still, God didn't give me what I deserved! I try hard to remind myself that God has feelings too. I hate being used by people, often times, I allow myself to be used, so I can relate to what God feels when we take, take, take, and rebel when He asks us to give. He loves us in a way that our minds will never be able to understand; however, we should take a little more time to consider Who He is and why we love Him. Consider being more considerate of God… now there's a thought!

Friends

Ever sit and think about how time passes you by...
As you ponder it all, you begin to analyze how much time you invested in fruitless relationships
No, you don't have to call every day to stay connected
Your spirits stay in tune, keeping you engaged
Even if you all are thousands of miles away from one another
Your heart remains connected to that sister or that brother
That friend
Don't apologize if you realize you may not have a connection with some
As you once thought
Friendships take time to be built
They are nurtured and cultivated
Solidified on solid ground
Friends are often brought to you
Rarely found
Intimately designed; chapters clearly defined
To make up the beautiful story that is you
Friends...

Friends Understand

That has always been one of my struggles... I afford people the title of friend too quickly. I'm 100% sure I am not the only one! I recognized something in myself that wasn't an easy pill to swallow and that was just how insecure I was. I felt like I needed the attention of people, I needed to be surrounded and I didn't realize that God's attention was the only attention that could fill the void I was trying to fill with "friendships." Now, don't get me wrong, I believe we are all supposed to have strong, healthy friendships to relate to, connect and commune with, but at the same time, the busyness of life will keep you from staying engaged consistently.

A strong friendship, built on a solid foundation, where you KNOW the path you're on with one another will survive. Love knows no distance. We have to learn how to be OK when people fall away, their priorities change and we have to be sure to remember, some folks are a part of your story's chapter and some are purposed to be there for the whole story. Know the difference.

Filled

We ask You, "Lord, fill me up with more of
You."
But yet, we don't make room for You to
We beg and plead to be more like You
Once the process begins, we fight to do what
"we" want to do
I bet You ask Yourself... why do you come to
Me if you still intend to do you?
Lord, I need for that to change…
I realize, the choice starts with me.
Change that tone, shift that path, and re-route
the course
I really do want to be filled to capacity with
You
I want to truly know Your Voice
That prayer we've all prayed, "Decrease me
that You might increase."
I want that to be reality for me…
Today

Emptied?

*I had someone tell me "You're stubborn and you
should be careful how many times you tell God no,
because one No from Him can change your entire life's
course…. so be careful with how quickly you spew your
No's to the Almighty." Of course, I rolled my eyes
and sucked my teeth with a snappy girl phrase playing
in my head of "Who do they think they're talking
to?" That was an indicator that there was truth to
what was spoken, because of the instant attitude I*

caught at the statement. I was the one, when moved emotionally, I'd be all in for God using all of the clichés, "Fill me up God," "Use me Lord," "Lead me O God," and God in His infinite wisdom already knew it was lip service.

I wanted those things in the moment because I was "feeling" it. What we fail to realize when we make those requests is the processing that comes with it. You want God to fill your heart with His desires for you, your heart has to be cleared out. You want God to use you, you have to make yourself available to be used and you have to be willing to be used in ANY capacity God calls you to, not what's convenient for you. You can't fill a vessel that isn't emptied... I am growing there, I've come a long way and I still have a ways to go. I realize in areas God has cleared out in my heart, what He desires for me is a million times better than what I'd planned for myself... that's the truth. Got to get emptied to be filled!

MY ISSUES

Envy -HAIKU

Your confidence I loathe
Because you know exactly
Who you are fully

Insecurely Me...

Wake up
Shower
Moisturize
Get Dressed
Comb Tresses
Line eyes, matte lips
Smoothing hands over hips
Clear mascara
No foundation today
Bronze those cheeks
Dare not miss a spot, I say…
Pass by the mirror one more time
Stop
Stare
Glare
Yep! She's still there
Behind the perfectly pressed hair
No matter how hard you stare
She is still there
She isn't going anywhere
The tear stains trace
The small lines of her face
That feeling of being out of place
"I don't like my face," her mind's voice
echoes
"I gotta be careful that not a hair is out of
place,"
Nobody has to know
I'll glue the pieces together to make it through
another day…
I can't let them see
They simply can't know

That I don't have it altogether
I've worked too hard to show otherwise
I've got to hide the pain, behind beautifully
made up eyes
Maybe they won't see
I pray they don't see
Insecurely me

Step 1…Removing The Mask

*One of the hardest parts of overcoming my insecurities
was acknowledging that I was insecure. I really
thought what was going on inside of me wasn't visible
to anyone else... boy did I learn! What happens on the
inside must come out. The stare downs I used to have
with myself in the mirror, I'm sure I offended God the
way my eyes expressed disdain for the reflection in
front of me.*

*However, when I acknowledge the weak areas about
me, what I didn't like, what I thought I needed to
change in order to like me… that's really when it all
changed for me. Overcoming my insecurities took all
of God and none of me, because if I had it my way, I
would've changed EVERYTHING… not realizing
I still would've been unhappy. God didn't snap His
Fingers and suddenly I changed, He was gradual but
potent. The closer I grew to Him, the more I begin to
love me. See, the closer you grow to God, the more you
learn about you. The intricacies of who you are, your
uniqueness, the beauty of you, your true essence.*

Arriving to that place starts with guess what? A choice, yep! It is really that simple… there is power in your choice. The insecurities of individuals didn't develop overnight, so it takes time to shed the layers, but once you do you begin to see a clearer day. Be mindful, it's not for you to live up to the perception others have made their personal reality concerning you. Your only job is to be grateful for who you are, how you were created, and open to growing into who God has called you to be. Take off that mask and set yourself free… live in peace, securely.

Dear Little Brown Girl

You're a pearl
Your skin, smooth and bright
Keep smiling beautiful
The darkness of this world needs your Light
Don't allow the shallow insecurities of others
Cause you to question your beauty
Lightening your skin to be like them
Tells God He made a mistake
No, oh no! No how, no way!
Dear Little Brown Girl
The gorgeousness of you
Started from deep within
The uniqueness of your spirit
Surfaces to the exterior
Highlighting that melanin
Bronzy, brown skin
Your heart, is big, and beats loud
With every beat of it, it's God's intent
To remind you that you're a beautiful gift
Not defined by the skin you're in
But by the way you Love
To the lengths you Love
And the destiny you hold within
In this letter to you I say
Dear Little Brown Girl
Go on about your way
Shaping paths
Making moves
Being the change the worlds needs to embrace
Teach everyone you see
To look beyond their vanity
Embracing the originality

We were all created in
You, them, him, her and me.

The Skin You're In is IN!

We all look in the mirror at ourselves, whether we're getting ready for the day or we're examining some imperfection of ourselves that we hope will fade away. It takes some time to really love the skin you're in, especially if you grew up without affirmation that you're beautiful the way you are. The poem was entitled Dear Little Brown Girl but the message ties to any person that has not yet accepted they are the perfect imperfection.

We live in a society that has taught people to think backwards, people taking care of the outside, but rotting away on the inside. Not realizing that when you age and the exterior beauty fades, your heart, your character, how you love, the compassion you show will be the legacy of you. I have never heard anyone say, "When I die, I want to be remembered for how beautiful my face was, how long my hair was, how pretty my teeth were." I hear people say things like, "I want to be remembered for the work I did, the changes God used me to make in the world."

This piece is a personal page out of my life's book... for years, I imagined bleaching my skin, veneering my teeth and I wanted to wear contacts, get liposuction, I just didn't like me, especially my dark skin. Boy am I thankful that God picked up His mirror to show me who I was and taught me through many of His messengers how to love who I am. It was a long road, but worth it to be traveled because now, I seek to empower young men and women all of over the world to love the skin they were created in. God was strategic in His unique approach to creating you and there is NO ONE IN THE WORLD like you... not a single soul. Think on that... for just a second... there is only one YOU... your genetic makeup is detailed and defined and there are no carbon copies. I'll tell you this to, once you learn to really love you it will make loving others much more easier to do.

Busy Body

Ms. Nosey
Cheeks rosy
Eyes bright
Dancing around
Looking for the next thing to get into
Oh girl, poor girl
How fooled your lust to know everybody
else's stuff has you
Tell this
Hear that
"Honey, I got some tea for you…"
Little do you realize…
With every gossiping lie
You dig a hole that God didn't mean for you
Mind your business girl
Your life has enough drama of its own
Stirred up pots, lead to burned up arms
Don't be fooled by the gossip's devilish
charm
Girl, oh girl…
I sure wish you would mind your own
Talking about folks business
Gonna leave you messed up and all alone
Have you stopped to think about how it
feels…
To those you talk about
What if that shoe is forced to fit on you?
Ms. Busy Body, what would you do?

Hey You Spilling That Tea… Wipe It Up!

I was sitting in a teaching one day, when the pastor said, "Those of y'all that's talking about folks, you know, that's in the Bible too?" I was like NO WAY! Well, I Googled and sure enough, there it was, as clear as day, "[41] For we hear that there are some who walk among you in a disorderly manner, not working at all, but are busybodies…" (1 Thessalonians 3:11).

I was convicted immediately! I didn't think what I was doing was considered gossiping as long as I was only talking to my "friends," boy did I learn! Gossip hurts people; we've all heard the scripture quoted, "Death and Life are in the power of the tongue and those who love it will eat its fruit," Proverbs 18:21, it's true. Every time I spoke on someone else's life without the facts, I spewed death into the atmosphere and I won't lie to you, I paid for it to. It does not pay to talk about folks, trust and believe it comes back on you.

My mama used to refer to folks that spoke on things that didn't concern them as busybodies and to read it in the Bible, I get in now for sure. I learned a huge life lesson from being a busy body for years, give life to others by speaking life over others. Talking about other people only revealed how insecure I truly was, when I learned to see the value in other people's lives, I began to see value in my own.

Mask

You wear it well
So no one can tell
What lies beneath
That mask
You've done some harm
Judge him
Judge her
Pick out all their flaws
Just make sure that mask you wear
Doesn't fall off
Show the world what you want them to see
While shoving more bones into your closet
daily
Don't you want to be free?
Remove the mask
See your truth for itself
Face the issues you placed on a shelf
Let the tears fall if they need to
Believe me when I say, God wants to heal you
Seriously, if He did it for me
He certainly will do it for you
But first you've got to take of the mask
So He can see you

Masquerade Ball... Right Before the Fall

*Today's society has set us up well, to wear masks of
various kinds, our faces covered perfectly, not a single
soul can tell... who we really are. I know this tale all
too well, I had a bevy of masks indeed. There was the
"I do nothing wrong, they do everything*

wrong" *mask then there was the* "I have it all together" *mask, those two were the most prevalent, but there were many more. I gave my life to Christ, for real, when I did, He began spiritual surgery on me. Every time I read His word, prayed and sought His Truth, He worked on me, worked stuff out of me. I remember the delayering process, you usually do remember the painful processes. I think that's intentional because if you remembered how much it hurt you're not likely to tread down that road again.*

It was HARD for me to admit that I was judgmental, hypocritical, envious of others, insecure, angry, hurt, and even unforgiving. Facing those blatant truths about me were reality indeed, but I've overcome many of those things and I continue to overcome because I faced them. I admitted to myself that those were my struggles, prayed to God, confessed that I am a mess and finally accepted that masks I wore God saw right through every day.

Here's something I realize, we go through the motions to "pretend" all is well and what good does it do us at the end of it all? I had to think, if God cracked that sky when I was faking it, who did it hurt when I was caught in that position, in that state? Me... not the people I was putting on for, not God... ME. I don't know about you, but I'd rather put the work in to really see change then to pretend I've changed and receive no reward. Pride is usually what keeps us putting on the mask every day; we all know what comes after pride slides in the door... the FALL. Do yourself a favor, take the masks off… show that beautiful face.

This page is intentionally left blank

About The Author

Stacy "Simply Stacy" Wilson is a passionate poet, author, motivational speaker, and visionary armed with a warm and infectious smile, along with a sincere desire to uplift and encourage others, Stacy's journey of using words to reach out to the world began.

About the Illustrator

Teenage artist, Sydney J. Wilson, discovered her passion for art four years ago. What started as a hobby developed into big dreams that she is on the path to realizing. Sydney's artistic imagination, ability to capture thought provoking emotions in the smallest details is what makes her art unique. The journey for Sydney has just begun, get ready world, she's on her way.

Connect With **Simply Stacy**

LIKE:
https://www.facebook.com/simplystacypoetry/
FOLLOW:
@FollowingHisWay
CONTACT:
simplystacypoetry@gmail.com
TEXT: (678) 856-7438

www.ingramcontent.com/pod-product-compliance
Lightning Source LLC
Chambersburg PA
CBHW050949030426
42339CB00007B/354